DIGITAL ARREST

A Survival Guide to Government Impersonation, Identity Theft, IRS & FBI Fraud

MANOJ KUMAR NAIR

BlueRose ONE.com DIY
Stories Matter
New Delhi • London

BLUEROSE PUBLISHERS
India | U.K.

For permissions requests or inquiries regarding this publication,
please contact:

BLUEROSE PUBLISHERS
www.BlueRoseONE.com
info@bluerosepublishers.com
+91 8882 898 898
+4407342408967

ISBN: 978-93-7825-276-1

First Edition: March 2026

Table of Contents

Introduction

When Fear Becomes a Weapon

It usually begins like any other day.

A phone rings while someone is driving to work, preparing breakfast, or sitting quietly at home. The number looks ordinary—sometimes even familiar. The voice on the other end sounds confident, authoritative, and calm. There is no shouting at first. No threats. Just a statement delivered with unsettling certainty:

"You are under investigation."

In that moment, life splits into two parts—**before the call and after the call**.

For the person receiving the call, nothing feels real anymore. The room feels smaller. The world narrows. Thoughts scatter. The voice continues, explaining that there has been suspicious activity linked to the person's identity, bank account, mobile number or digital footprint. The caller claims to represent the police, a cybercrime unit, a government authority or an international agency. They know details—your name, your phone number, sometimes even your address. Enough to sound convincing. Enough to sound dangerous.

And then comes the instruction: *do not disconnect the call.*

This is how a Digital Arrest begins.

Not with handcuffs.
Not with police sirens.
But with **fear delivered through a phone**.

A New Kind of Crime, A New Kind of Prison

In the physical world, an arrest is visible. There are procedures, paperwork, safeguards and witnesses. There is at least the comfort of knowing where you stand, who is accusing you and what your rights are.

A digital arrest has none of these.

It happens silently, privately and quickly. The victim is isolated—mentally first, then emotionally, and finally financially. The scammer creates an invisible prison where the victim believes they are being watched, recorded, and evaluated at every moment. Video calls are used to maintain control. Fake uniforms, official backdrops, forged documents, and legal jargon reinforce the illusion of authority.

The victim is told not to contact family members, lawyers, or colleagues. Any attempt to seek help is framed as "non-cooperation" or "obstruction of justice." Fear replaces logic. Urgency replaces reason.

And before the victim fully understands what has happened, money has already changed hands.

Sometimes lifetime savings.
Sometimes retirement funds.
Sometimes borrowed money.

Always real.

"I Never Thought This Could Happen to Me"

Almost every victim says the same thing.

"I am educated."
"I work in a reputed company."
"I understand technology."
"I am careful with money."

Yet cyber fraud does not discriminate by intelligence, profession, or social status.

Doctors, engineers, teachers, business owners, retired government officials, homemakers, students—people from every background have fallen victim to Digital Arrest scams. Many of them had previously warned others about online fraud. Some had attended cybersecurity awareness programs. Some had even laughed at scam messages in the past.

So why does it still work?

Because this is not a technology problem.
It is a **human psychology problem**.

Cybercriminals do not hack systems first. They hack **emotions**.

Fear.
Shame.
Authority.
Urgency.
Isolation.

These are the tools of modern cyber fraud.

The Silence After the Scam

The money loss is devastating—but the emotional damage often goes deeper.

Victims struggle with shame. Many do not report the crime immediately, fearing judgment from family members or colleagues. Some worry they will be blamed for being careless. Others fear legal trouble, believing the scammer's final warning that "going to the police will make things worse."

This silence is exactly what cybercriminals rely on.

The longer the delay, the harder it becomes to trace the money. The psychological trauma lingers. Trust erodes—not just in technology, but in people, institutions, and even oneself.

Some victims experience anxiety, insomnia, depression, and withdrawal. Families are affected. Relationships are strained. In extreme cases, the emotional aftermath has led to severe mental health crises.

Yet outside their personal world, life goes on. The scammer moves on to the next call. The system records another statistic. The story disappears.

This book exists to break that silence.

Why This Book Had to Be Written

Digital Arrest scams are not isolated incidents. They are part of a **global, organized cybercrime ecosystem** that is growing faster than public awareness.

Every year, billions of dollars are lost worldwide to frauds that rely not on malware, but on manipulation. Technology has given criminals reach, speed, and anonymity. Artificial intelligence, deepfake technology, and voice cloning are making scams more convincing than ever before.

Meanwhile, ordinary people are expected to navigate this complex digital world with limited guidance, outdated awareness campaigns, and the false belief that "it won't happen to me."

This book was written to challenge that belief.

This book is a **guide for ordinary people living in an extraordinary digital age**.

A Final Word Before You Continue

Some chapters ahead may feel uncomfortable to read. You may recognize situations that feel close to home. You may think of someone you know who could be vulnerable. You may even recall a moment when you narrowly avoided such a call—or did not.

That discomfort is not weakness. It is awareness forming.

If this book helps even one person pause before transferring money, question a threatening call, or seek help without shame, it has served its purpose.

Digital arrests are not real—but their consequences are.

Let this book be the moment when fear loses its power.

Let this be the point where knowledge takes its place.

Chapter 1

The Call That Changes Everything

The phone vibrates on the table while Rajesh is halfway through his morning coffee. The news plays softly in the background. His phone screen lights up with an unfamiliar number, but it looks local. No international code. No warning signs. He hesitates for a second, then answers.

"Hello?"

There is a brief pause on the other end, followed by a calm, authoritative voice.

"Good morning. Is this Mr. Rajesh Kumar?"

Something about the tone makes him sit up straighter. It is not aggressive. Not hurried. Just confident. Controlled.

"Yes," he replies. "Who is this?"

"I am calling from the Cyber Crime Department. This call is being recorded. Please listen carefully and do not interrupt."

Rajesh's stomach tightens.

In the space of a few seconds, the room feels quieter. The television noise fades into the background. His coffee grows cold in his hand. He tells himself there must be some mistake. He has done nothing wrong. He barely uses social media. He pays his taxes. He is careful.

But the voice continues.

"Your Aadhaar number and mobile number have been linked to multiple suspicious transactions. This matter is serious. Are you aware of this?"

Rajesh's mind races.

Suspicious transactions? Linked to what? How? When?

"No… no, I don't know anything about this," he says, his voice suddenly unsure.

"That is exactly why we are calling," the voice replies calmly. "If you cooperate, this can be resolved. But if you do not, the consequences will be severe."

This is the moment where fear quietly enters the room.

The First Crack in Reality

Fear does not arrive loudly. It slips in gently, disguised as confusion.

Rajesh thinks of his bank account. His family. His job. His reputation. He tries to remember if he has ever clicked a suspicious link, ignored a warning message, or shared personal details. The more he thinks, the more uncertain he becomes.

The caller knows this.

He explains that a parcel containing illegal items has been intercepted. Rajesh's identity has been used. There is talk of money laundering, fake accounts, international networks. The words blur together, but they all point in one direction: trouble.

"We believe your identity has been misused," the caller says. "But until verification is complete, you are considered under investigation."

Under investigation.

The words carry weight. They sound official. Dangerous.

Rajesh asks the question that most victims ask at this point.

"What should I do?"

The answer comes immediately.

"You must stay available on this call. Do not discuss this with anyone. Do not contact a lawyer. Do not visit the police station. If you alert anyone prematurely, the case will escalate."

Rajesh nods instinctively, even though the caller cannot see him.

This is the first invisible wall of the digital arrest.

Isolation.

When Authority Feels Absolute

The call is transferred.

A video request appears on Rajesh's phone. The caller explains that a senior officer will now speak to him. Rajesh hesitates, but fear pushes him forward. He accepts.

The screen lights up.

A man in uniform appears. The background looks official—framed certificates, a flag, a desk. The man's expression is serious but controlled. He introduces himself with a title Rajesh has heard before, one associated with power and law.

"Mr. Rajesh," the officer says, "this is not a small matter. Your cooperation will determine how this proceeds."

Rajesh feels something shift inside him.

This is no longer just a phone call. This feels real. The uniform. The setting. The confidence. The legal language.

The officer explains that to prevent immediate arrest, Rajesh must undergo a "digital verification process." His accounts need to be checked. His financial history must be reviewed. This is described as a protective step, something that will help prove his innocence.

"But understand this," the officer adds. "During this process, you are under digital arrest. You must remain available and follow instructions strictly."

Digital arrest.

Rajesh has never heard the term before, but it makes sense in the moment. Everything is digital now—banking, documents, work. Why not arrests?

Fear fills the gaps where logic should be.

The Psychology of Compliance

At this stage, Rajesh is no longer thinking clearly.

His heart is beating faster. His mouth feels dry. His thoughts jump between worst-case scenarios. Arrest. Public embarrassment. Losing his job. His family finding out.

The scammers understand this state perfectly.

They do not rush him. They do not shout. They maintain calm authority. They reassure him that cooperation will protect him. They warn him that delay will harm him.

This balance of fear and reassurance is intentional.

Rajesh is asked to show his ID on camera. Then his bank details "for verification." He hesitates briefly, but the officer reminds him that refusal will be noted as non-cooperation.

"No genuine person refuses verification," the officer says quietly.

Rajesh complies.

He tells himself this is temporary. That it will end soon. That he just needs to get through this.

That is how people surrender control—not all at once, but step by step.

The Moment Money Enters the Story

The conversation shifts.

The officer explains that suspicious funds may have passed through Rajesh's account. To separate legitimate money from illegal funds, a temporary transfer is required. The money will be returned once verification is complete.

Rajesh's instincts scream that this is wrong.

But fear speaks louder.

"What if I don't have that amount?" Rajesh asks.

"There are procedures," the officer replies. "But refusal will complicate your case."

Rajesh looks at his bank balance. It is money saved over years. For emergencies. For his children's education. For peace of mind.

This now feels like an emergency.

He transfers the money.

The confirmation message arrives instantly.

The officer nods. "Good. You are cooperating."

Relief floods Rajesh's body.

For a brief moment, he believes he has done the right thing.

The Endless Loop

But the call does not end.

New issues arise. Additional verifications are required. More discrepancies are discovered. Each one requires another step, another transfer, another assurance.

Rajesh's world has shrunk to the size of his phone screen.

He does not eat. He does not step outside. He does not answer other calls. He is told to stay visible on video. To keep his phone charged. To respond immediately.

This is the digital cell.

No bars. No locks. Just fear and obedience.

Hours pass.

When Rajesh finally questions the process, the officer's tone changes slightly.

"Are you trying to escape investigation?"

The word escape terrifies him.

"No, no," Rajesh says quickly. "I am cooperating."

And so it continues.

The Silence After

Eventually, the call ends.

The officer promises that the case is under review and that Rajesh will be contacted again.

The screen goes dark.

The silence in the room is deafening.

Rajesh looks around as if waking from a nightmare. His phone shows no missed calls from real authorities. No official messages. Just bank alerts.

Only then does the truth begin to surface.

He tries calling the number back.

It does not exist.

The Real Arrest

The real arrest does not happen with police.

It happens in the mind.

Rajesh sits frozen, staring at his phone, replaying every moment of the call. Every word. Every decision. His hands shake. His chest feels tight.

He realizes what has happened.

The money is gone.

Shame crashes over him like a wave.

How could he fall for this?
Why didn't he hang up?
Why didn't he call someone?

He thinks of telling his family—and cannot. He thinks of going to the police—and hesitates. He thinks of being judged—and stays silent.

This is the final victory of the scammer.

Not the money.

The silence.

Why This Story Matters

Rajesh is not alone.

Every day, thousands of people across the world receive similar calls. Different names. Different accents. Same script. Same outcome.

This chapter is not about blaming victims. It is about understanding how easily fear can override logic when authority is weaponized.

If you see yourself in Rajesh's story, remember this:

You are not weak.
You are human.

And once you understand how this works, it becomes much harder to fall into the same trap.

In the next chapter, we will break down what a Digital Arrest really is—and why no real authority has the power to do this over a phone call.

But for now, remember this moment.

The moment the phone rings.

That is where everything begins.

Chapter 2

What Is a Digital Arrest?

There is a moment—usually hours or days after the call—when the words begin to sound strange.

"Digital arrest."

Victims replay the phrase in their minds, trying to understand it. At the time of the call, it felt logical. Everything else in life is digital now—banking, payments, work meetings, documents, signatures, surveillance. Why wouldn't law enforcement also operate digitally?

But once the fear settles and the silence grows, the question finally surfaces:

Is digital arrest even a real thing?

The answer is simple.

No.

There is no such legal concept.

And that is precisely why it works.

The Power of a Made-Up Term

Digital arrest is not defined in any law book. It does not exist in criminal procedure. No police department, cybercrime unit, or government agency has the authority to arrest someone over a phone call, video call, or messaging app.

Yet thousands of people across the world believe they have been arrested digitally.

Not because the law allows it—but because **fear convinces them it must be true**.

Scammers create this term deliberately. It sounds official enough to intimidate, modern enough to feel relevant, and vague enough to avoid scrutiny. It lives in a grey area where victims do not feel confident enough to question it.

Most people are not legal experts. They do not know exact procedures. They only know one thing: getting into trouble with the law is terrifying.

Cybercriminals exploit that uncertainty.

Arrest Without Handcuffs

A traditional arrest is a physical event.

There are officers. Documents. A location. Witnesses. A timeline. There is clarity, even if the situation is frightening.

A digital arrest removes all of that.

There are no papers to read.
No badges to verify.
No offices to visit.

Everything happens inside the victim's head.

The scammer does not need to restrain the body. They only need to restrain the **mind**.

The moment a victim accepts the idea that they are "under investigation" or "under digital arrest," their behavior changes instantly. They stop questioning. They stop thinking independently. They start obeying.

This is not accidental. It is psychological conditioning.

Why the Brain Freezes Under Authority

Human beings are wired to respect authority.

From childhood, we are taught that police, courts, and government agencies represent power, order, and consequences. We are told that non-cooperation leads to punishment. This conditioning runs deep, often deeper than logic.

When a calm, confident voice claims authority and uses legal language, the brain does not pause to verify facts. It reacts emotionally.

Heart rate increases.
Stress hormones flood the body.
The rational part of the brain slows down.

This is why victims later say, “I don’t know what I was thinking.”

They were thinking—but under fear.

A digital arrest thrives in this mental state.

The Illusion of Surveillance

One of the most powerful elements of a digital arrest scam is the feeling of being watched.

Victims are often told:

- “This call is being recorded.”
- “Your activities are under surveillance.”
- “We can see your transactions in real time.”
- “Do not disconnect the call.”

Sometimes video calls are used to reinforce this illusion. The victim believes their movements, expressions, and reactions are being monitored. They begin to self-police their behavior.

They sit still.
They speak carefully.
They comply quickly.

This is not law enforcement.

This is psychological captivity.

Why Victims Don’t Question the Process

Looking back, people often wonder why victims did not simply hang up.

The answer lies in how the scam unfolds.

Scammers do not begin with threats. They begin with information.

Your name.
Your phone number.
Sometimes your address or workplace.

This creates credibility. Once credibility is established, authority follows. Once authority is accepted, instructions are obeyed.

By the time money is mentioned, the victim is already emotionally invested. Hanging up now feels dangerous. Disobeying feels risky. Continuing feels safer—even when it is not.

Digital arrest is not about logic. It is about momentum.

Isolation Is the Key Ingredient

One rule is emphasized above all others:

"Do not tell anyone."

Victims are warned that involving family, friends, lawyers, or even local police will worsen the situation. This instruction serves one purpose: isolation.

Isolation removes external reality checks.

A single conversation with a trusted person is often enough to break the illusion. Scammers know this. That is why secrecy is framed as cooperation.

The victim is made to believe that silence is protection.

In truth, silence is surrender.

No Due Process, No Rights

Real legal processes are slow, structured, and transparent. They involve notices, summons, written communication, and opportunities to respond.

A digital arrest has none of this.

There is no documentation sent through official channels.
No time given to verify claims.
No chance to consult anyone.

Everything is urgent. Everything is immediate. Everything happens now.

Urgency is not a legal requirement.

It is a manipulation tactic.

The Role of Fear in Decision-Making

Fear does something dangerous: it shortens time.

Under fear, the future collapses into the present moment. Long-term consequences disappear. The only goal becomes stopping the immediate threat.

That is why victims transfer money they had saved for years.

That is why they ignore obvious red flags.

That is why they comply with instructions they would normally question.

The scammer does not need to convince the victim that the process is legitimate. They only need to convince them that **delay is dangerous**.

Digital arrest lives in that narrow window.

Why the Term Feels Believable Today

Ten years ago, this scam would not have worked as well.

But today, we live in a world where:

- Court hearings happen over video calls
- Documents are signed digitally
- Bank accounts are frozen online

- Surveillance is openly discussed
- Work happens remotely

Digital authority feels normal.

So when someone claims that legal action can also be digital, the brain does not reject it immediately.

Scammers have adapted their language to the times.

The law has not—but fear fills the gap.

The Moment of Realization

For most victims, realization comes quietly.

A number does not connect.
A promised call never comes.
A bank balance does not recover.

And slowly, painfully, the truth emerges.

There was no case.
No investigation.
No officer.
No arrest.

Only manipulation.

This realization is often accompanied by intense self-blame. Victims replay conversations repeatedly, searching for the moment where everything went wrong.

But the truth is uncomfortable:

The scam did not succeed because the victim was careless.
It succeeded because the scam was designed to succeed.

Naming the Crime Matters

Calling this a "digital arrest" scam is important—not because the term is real, but because it exposes the lie.

Once named, it can be recognized.

Once recognized, it can be resisted.

This chapter exists to dismantle the illusion completely.

There is no such thing as a digital arrest. There is only psychological coercion delivered through technology.

What Comes Next

Now that you understand what a digital arrest truly is—and what it is not—the next step is to understand **why intelligent, capable people still fall for it**.

In the next chapter, we will explore the psychological triggers that override common sense, and why education alone is not enough to protect against fear-based fraud.

Because awareness is not just knowing the rules.

It is understanding the mind.

And once you understand that, fear loses its grip.

Chapter 3

Why Smart People Fall for It

When the story finally comes out, there is often an awkward silence.

Someone listens carefully as the victim explains what happened—the call, the officer, the threats, the transfers. And then comes the question that stings more than the loss itself:

"How could you fall for that?"

It is usually asked without cruelty. Sometimes with disbelief. Sometimes with genuine confusion. But always with an assumption hiding beneath it—that intelligence should have been enough.

That assumption is wrong.

Cyber fraud does not target stupidity. It targets **human psychology**.

And psychology does not care how educated you are.

Intelligence Is Not Immunity

There is a comforting belief many people hold:

"I am too smart for this to happen to me."

It feels reassuring. Protective. Logical.

But it is also dangerous.

Because intelligence helps when you have time to think. Digital arrest scams are designed to ensure you do not.

Victims often include:

- Engineers who design complex systems
- Doctors trained to make life-or-death decisions
- Lawyers who understand the law

- Business owners who negotiate high-value deals
- IT professionals who work in cybersecurity

These are not careless people.

They are people placed under **extreme emotional pressure**.

The Myth of Rational Decision-Making

We like to believe that humans make decisions rationally.

We don't.

Most decisions—especially under stress—are emotional first, rational second.

When fear enters the body, it triggers a survival response. Heart rate increases. Breathing changes. Stress hormones flood the system. The brain shifts control away from thoughtful analysis and toward quick reaction.

This is not a flaw.

It is biology.

Cybercriminals do not fight this response. They trigger it intentionally.

Authority Bias: The Oldest Trick Still Works

Authority bias is the tendency to comply with figures who appear to hold power.

Uniforms. Titles. Official language. Structured speech.

These signals bypass skepticism.

From childhood, we are conditioned to obey authority. Teachers. Police. Officials. Institutions. We are taught that questioning authority leads to consequences.

Digital arrest scams exploit this conditioning perfectly.

The scammer does not need to prove authority. They only need to **perform it convincingly**.

Once the victim accepts the role of "citizen under investigation," obedience follows naturally.

Fear Shrinks the World

Under fear, the world becomes small.

The future disappears. The past feels irrelevant. Only the present moment matters.

Victims stop thinking about:

- Long-term consequences
- Financial stability
- Verification steps

They start thinking about:

- Ending the call safely
- Avoiding arrest
- Protecting reputation

This tunnel vision is not stupidity.

It is survival mode.

The Power of Legal Language

Most people are not fluent in legal procedures.

Scammers know this.

They use complex terms—case numbers, sections, jurisdictions—not to inform, but to overwhelm. When language becomes confusing, people stop asking questions.

Confusion creates dependence.

The victim begins to rely on the scammer to guide them through the "process."

This is not guidance.

It is control.

Shame as a Silencing Tool

Shame plays a critical role before and after the scam.

Before the scam, shame is used to isolate: "If this becomes public, your reputation will be destroyed."

After the scam, shame keeps victims silent: "I should have known better."

Shame prevents reporting.
Shame prevents recovery.
Shame protects the criminal.

Smart people often experience deeper shame because their identity is tied to competence.

Admitting vulnerability feels like admitting failure.

Urgency Destroys Verification

Every digital arrest scam includes urgency.

"This must be done now."
"Delay will worsen your case."
"Non-cooperation will be recorded."

Urgency eliminates second opinions.

There is no time to Google.
No time to call a friend.
No time to think.

The victim is rushed forward before doubt can form.

Urgency is not legal.

It is manipulative.

The Illusion of Partial Control

Scammers often allow victims to make small choices:

- Which account to use
- What time to transfer
- How to stay connected

This creates an illusion of control.

The victim feels involved, not trapped.

But the outcome is already decided.

Cognitive Overload and Compliance

As the call continues, information piles up.

New problems. New steps. New instructions.

The brain becomes overloaded.

When mental capacity is exceeded, people default to compliance.

"Just tell me what to do."

This is not surrender.

It is exhaustion.

Why Education Alone Is Not Enough

Awareness campaigns often focus on facts: "Police will never ask for money."

Facts are important—but they are not enough.

Under fear, facts are inaccessible.

The part of the brain that recalls information is suppressed when stress is high. This is why victims later say, "I knew this—but I forgot."

They didn't forget.

They were overridden.

The Role of Trust in Modern Life

Modern life requires trust.

We trust digital payments. Online services. Remote communication. Official emails. Video calls.

Scammers hide inside this trust.

They do not appear unusual—they appear normal.

Questioning everything is not realistic.

That is why targeted manipulation is so effective.

The Moment Logic Returns

Logic returns slowly.

Usually after the call ends.
After the pressure lifts.
After silence arrives.

Then questions appear:
"Why would police ask for money?"
"Why couldn't I tell anyone?"
"Why was everything so urgent?"

By then, the damage is done.

This delay is intentional.

Reframing the Narrative

Victims must stop asking:
"Why was I so stupid?"

And start asking:
"How was I manipulated?"

This shift matters.

Blame keeps people silent.
Understanding empowers them.

Intelligence Plus Awareness Is Power

Smart people fall for digital arrest scams not because they lack intelligence, but because intelligence alone is not designed to fight emotional manipulation.

The real defense is:

- Awareness of psychological triggers
- Permission to pause
- Willingness to question authority
- Courage to seek help

In the next chapter, we will dissect the scam script step by step—not to admire its effectiveness, but to dismantle it.

Because once you see the pattern, it loses its power.

And once fear loses its power, so do the scammers.

Chapter 4

The Scam Script: Step by Step

Every Digital Arrest scam feels personal.

Victims often believe they were targeted specifically—that the caller knew something unique, that the timing was unlucky, that the situation was extraordinary.

It wasn't.

What happened to them followed a **script**.

Not a rough outline.
Not an improvisation.
A practiced, refined, repeatable script—tested on

thousands of people across countries, languages, and cultures.

This chapter breaks that script apart, not to glorify its effectiveness, but to strip it of its power.

Because once you see the steps clearly, the illusion collapses.

Step 1: The First Contact — Calm, Not Aggressive

Contrary to popular belief, Digital Arrest scams rarely begin with shouting or threats.

They begin calmly.

The caller introduces themselves politely, often using a full name and designation. The tone is professional, measured, and authoritative. The goal at this stage is **credibility**, not fear.

Anonymized case:
A 42-year-old finance manager received a call during office hours from a man who spoke calmly and addressed him by full name. The caller stated he was "verifying information related to a cyber complaint." No accusations were made initially.

This stage is about lowering defenses.

If the opening feels too aggressive, people hang up. Calmness signals legitimacy.

Step 2: Establishing Authority and Stakes

Once the victim stays on the line, the caller introduces authority.

They reference:

- Police departments
- Cybercrime units
- Government agencies
- International enforcement bodies

They may mention case numbers, sections of law, or technical terms. Accuracy is not important. Confidence is.

Then come the stakes.

Words like:

- “Serious matter”
- “Under investigation”
- “Non-bailable offense”
- “International implications”

Fear is introduced—but gently.

The victim is unsettled, not panicked.

That comes later.

Step 3: Personalization Through Partial Information

The scammer now reveals limited personal details:

- Name
- Phone number
- Sometimes address or ID reference

This information is often sourced from data leaks, public databases, or previous scams.

To the victim, it feels invasive.

"If they know this much, they must be real."

That assumption is exactly what the scam depends on.

Anonymized case:
A retired government employee reported that the caller quoted the last four digits of his identification number. Later investigation showed the data came from a leaked database unrelated to any crime.

The information does not prove guilt.

It proves access.

Step 4: Creating a Narrative of Risk

Now the story begins.

The victim is told that:

- Their identity has been misused
- A parcel or account is linked to illegal activity
- Their number appears in a criminal investigation

Details are vague but alarming.

The scammer avoids specifics that can be easily verified. The narrative is designed to be *plausible*, not provable.

This ambiguity forces the victim to imagine worst-case scenarios.

Fear fills the gaps.

Step 5: Introducing "Help" as Control

At this point, the scammer shifts roles.

They are no longer just an authority figure. They become a guide.

"You are cooperating."
"This can be resolved."
"We are here to help you."

This is a critical psychological pivot.

The scammer positions themselves as both threat and solution.

The victim begins to trust them—not because they want to, but because they feel they must.

Step 6: Isolation — The Most Important Step

One instruction becomes non-negotiable:

"Do not tell anyone."

This includes:

- Family
- Friends
- Lawyers
- Bank staff

- Local police

The justification varies:

- “It will cause panic”
- “It will alert other suspects”
- “It will complicate the case”

In reality, this instruction protects only one party: the scammer.

Anonymized case:
A software engineer remained on a continuous video call for over six hours because he was told disconnecting would be recorded as an attempt to flee investigation.

Isolation removes external reality checks.

Without isolation, the scam collapses.

Step 7: Escalation to a “Senior Officer”

Once fear and isolation are established, the call is escalated.

A new person joins:

- Higher rank

- More confidence
- More authority

Sometimes via video call.

Uniforms may be worn. Official-looking backdrops are used. The victim is told this escalation proves seriousness.

It does—but not in the way they think.

This is theater.

Step 8: The Term "Digital Arrest" Appears

Now the invented term enters the conversation.

"You are under digital arrest."
"You must remain available."
"You are being monitored."

The victim may hesitate—but by now, resistance is low.

The term sounds modern. Official. Logical.

The scammer explains rules:

- Stay on call
- Keep camera on

- Respond immediately
- Do not leave location

These rules create **psychological confinement**.

No handcuffs required.

Step 9: Verification Becomes Financial

Money is not mentioned until now—for a reason.

Once mentioned, it is framed as:

- Verification
- Security deposit
- Temporary transfer
- Clearance process

The scammer insists the money will be returned.

This is critical.

If the victim believed the money was gone forever, they might resist. Temporary loss feels acceptable under fear.

Anonymized case:
A small business owner transferred funds believing

they would be “reversed within two hours after audit completion.” No such audit existed.

Step 10: The First Transfer — Breaking the Barrier

The first transfer is the hardest.

After that, it gets easier.

Psychologically, once a person has crossed the line, they are more likely to continue to justify their actions rather than accept they made a mistake.

This is known as commitment bias.

The scammer knows this.

Step 11: Continuous Justification and Delays

After the transfer, the scammer does not disappear.

New issues are discovered. New discrepancies arise. More transfers are needed.

Each one is justified logically.

The victim is exhausted but compliant.

They are told:
"You are almost done."
"Just one more step."

This stage can last hours—or days.

Step 12: Disappearance

Eventually, the scam ends abruptly.

The call drops.
The number stops working.
Messages go unanswered.

The silence is shocking.

The victim realizes something is wrong—but denial often delays acceptance.

Step 13: The Aftermath

The realization is devastating.

Victims experience:

- Shock
- Shame
- Panic

- Self-blame

Many delay reporting. Some never report at all.

This delay benefits the scammer.

Why This Script Works So Well

Every step serves a purpose.

Nothing is random.

Calm creates trust.
Authority creates obedience.
Fear creates urgency.
Isolation removes resistance.
Money becomes inevitable.

The scam is not clever because of technology.

It is clever because it understands **people**.

Breaking the Script

The good news is simple:

This script fails the moment one step is interrupted.

Hanging up.
Calling someone.

Pausing.
Verifying independently.

That is all it takes.

In the next chapter, we will examine the tools scammers use—technology, fake documents, video calls—to bring this script to life.

Because understanding the tools makes the script impossible to perform. And once the performance fails, the scam collapses.

Chapter 5

Tools of Fear: The Technology Behind the Scam

When victims describe what happened to them, they rarely begin with technology.

They talk about how real it felt.

They remember the voice that sounded official.
The face on the screen that wore a uniform.
The documents that appeared instantly.
The confidence with which every instruction was delivered.

Technology, in a Digital Arrest scam, is not the crime itself.

It is the stage on which the crime is performed.

The real weapon is fear—but technology gives that fear shape, authority, and speed.

When Technology Becomes a Costume

We tend to associate cybercrime with sophistication—hackers breaking into systems, malware infecting devices, passwords being cracked.

Digital Arrest scams are different.

They rarely involve hacking at all.

Instead, they rely on something far simpler and far more powerful: **belief**.

Technology is used not to break systems, but to convince human beings that what they are experiencing is legitimate. It becomes a costume worn by the scammer, one that looks official enough to silence doubt.

The tools themselves are ordinary. Most are available to anyone with a smartphone and an internet connection. What makes them dangerous is not what they do—but *when* and *how* they are used.

The Phone Call That Looks Normal

The scam almost always begins with a phone call that appears unremarkable.

The number looks local. Sometimes it resembles an official helpline. Occasionally, a department name even appears on the screen.

The victim assumes this must mean something.

It doesn't.

Caller identification is not proof of identity. It is merely information displayed on a screen—information that can be manipulated with ease. Scammers exploit this blind trust in what we see.

When the phone rings and looks legitimate, most people answer without hesitation.

That single moment of trust is enough.

Voices Without Faces, Faces Without Authority

The voice on the call sounds professional. Calm. Confident. Not rushed. Not threatening—at least not yet.

This is intentional.

A raised voice creates resistance. A calm voice creates compliance.

Scammers train themselves to sound composed, authoritative, and reassuring. Some read from carefully written scripts. Others practice endlessly until the delivery feels natural.

And then, at the right moment, the call escalates into a video interaction.

This is where fear deepens.

Seeing a face triggers a powerful psychological response. The human brain is wired to trust what it can see. A uniform on a screen feels like proof. An official-looking background feels like legitimacy.

But video is not verification.

It is theater.

The Illusion of the Office

Victims often describe the setting on the screen: a desk, framed certificates, flags, official insignia, sometimes even other people moving in the background.

Some scammers create physical sets. Others rely on virtual backgrounds. Many combine both.

The result is convincing enough to stop questions from forming.

In that moment, the victim does not think to ask why a real officer would need to prove authority visually. Fear answers that question before logic can.

Once the image is accepted, the mind fills in the rest.

Documents That Arrive Too Quickly

One of the most unsettling moments for victims is when documents appear instantly.

Notices. Case summaries. Legal warnings.

They look formal. They use official language. They carry logos and seals.

And they are never meant to be examined closely.

The scammer rushes past them.

"You don't need to read this now."
"This is just for your record."
"We will explain later."

Speed is essential. The faster the document appears, the more real the situation feels. The victim assumes such efficiency must belong to an official system.

In reality, these documents are props—created once and reused endlessly.

Screen Sharing and Silent Control

In some cases, scammers ask victims to share their screen.

The excuse varies: verification, confirmation, audit.

The real purpose is control.

Once the screen is shared, the victim becomes cautious. They hesitate to search online. They avoid opening other apps. They fear being seen doing the "wrong" thing.

This is not surveillance.

It is intimidation.

The scammer does not need to watch closely. The victim polices themselves.

Messaging Apps and the Illusion of Continuity

After the initial call, communication often moves to messaging platforms.

This shift feels natural. Convenient. Professional.

Messages arrive promptly. Language remains formal. Official logos are used as profile pictures. The conversation continues seamlessly.

The victim begins to believe they are inside a legitimate case process.

But no real investigation unfolds over chat messages.

This continuity exists only to maintain psychological pressure.

Banking Technology: Speed Without Safety

Modern banking is designed for convenience.

Instant transfers. Real-time alerts. Seamless confirmations.

In a Digital Arrest scam, these features become weapons.

The victim is told that cooperation must be immediate. The scammer claims they can see transactions in real time. Every second matters.

The banking system does exactly what it was designed to do.

And fear does the rest.

"This Call Is Being Recorded"

Few phrases are more effective.

When victims hear this, they change their behavior instantly. They speak carefully. They answer quickly. They avoid asking questions.

Recording creates a sense of permanence. A belief that every word can be used against them.

In reality, the recording—if it exists at all—serves only one purpose: obedience.

Why None of This Feels Suspicious in the Moment

Looking back, victims often say the signs were obvious.

But during the scam, nothing feels obvious.

That is because multiple tools are used simultaneously.

A call.
A video.
A message.
A document.
A banking alert.

The brain becomes overloaded.

When overwhelmed, people stop analyzing and start following instructions. This is not weakness. It is how humans cope under pressure.

The scammer does not rely on a single tool.

They rely on **stacking** tools until resistance collapses.

Technology as a Confidence Trick

Every technological element in a Digital Arrest scam exists for one reason: to make the lie feel solid.

Not perfect.
Not flawless.
Just believable long enough.

A uniform does not create authority.
A document does not create legality.
A video does not create truth.

But when fear is present, they feel like they do.

What Real Authority Never Needs

Real law enforcement does not rely on intimidation.

It does not demand secrecy.
It does not require constant video presence.
It does not ask for money to prove innocence.

Real authority operates through procedure, not pressure.

Understanding this distinction is critical.

Taking the Mask Off

Once you see these tools for what they are, they lose their power.

A call is just a call.
A video is just an image.
A document is just a file.

Technology does not make something legal.

Only process does.

In the next chapter, we will follow what happens after fear succeeds—how money is moved, hidden, and made nearly impossible to recover.

Because once money enters the story, the illusion ends. And the consequences become painfully real.

Chapter 6

The Money Trap

Money enters the story quietly.

There is no dramatic demand at first. No outright threat. No obvious extortion. The request is framed carefully, wrapped in procedure, legality, and reassurance.

"This is only temporary."
"This will be returned after verification."
"This is for your own protection."

By the time money is mentioned, fear has already done its work.

The victim is no longer deciding freely. They are responding.

When Fear Makes Money Feel Secondary

In normal circumstances, money represents effort, security, and future plans. People guard it carefully. They question anyone who asks for it.

But under fear, money changes meaning.

It becomes a tool to end the threat.

The victim is no longer thinking, *"Can I afford this?"*
They are thinking, *"How do I make this stop?"*

This shift is critical.

The scammer does not need to convince the victim that the request makes sense—only that refusing it is dangerous.

The Language of Legitimacy

Scammers never say, "Send us your money."

They say:

- "Transfer funds for verification"

- “Secure your account temporarily”
- “Separate legitimate funds from suspicious ones”
- “Show cooperation”

These phrases are chosen carefully.

They sound procedural. Technical. Reasonable.

The victim does not feel robbed. They feel processed.

Why the Money Comes So Late

If money were requested at the beginning, most people would hang up.

That is why it appears only after:

- Authority is established
- Isolation is enforced
- Urgency is created

By then, the victim is emotionally invested.

They want the problem to end.
They want their innocence confirmed.
They want their life back.

Money becomes the price of relief.

"It Will Come Back"

This is the most dangerous promise.

Victims are told the transfer is temporary. That it will be reversed once verification is complete. That it is a technical formality.

This reassurance lowers resistance.

People are far more willing to risk money they believe they will get back.

The scammer understands this instinct.

What is never explained is how the money would be returned, or why a legitimate authority would need personal funds at all.

Fear answers those questions instead.

The First Transfer

The first transfer is the hardest.

The victim hesitates. They feel a knot in their stomach. Something feels wrong.

The scammer senses this.

They escalate urgency.
They question cooperation.
They hint at consequences.

Eventually, the victim complies.

And something important changes.

Once the first transfer is made, the psychological barrier is broken.

Commitment and Justification

After the first transfer, the victim feels an intense need to justify their decision.

Admitting a mistake now would be unbearable.

So they continue.

This is not greed.
It is self-protection.

The scammer relies on this.

Each additional transfer feels easier than admitting the first was wrong.

Banking as a Silent Accomplice

Modern banking systems are fast and efficient.

Transfers happen instantly. Confirmations arrive immediately. Alerts flash on the screen.

To the victim, this feels official.

To the scammer, it is perfect.

Speed prevents reflection. Efficiency prevents doubt.

The system works exactly as designed—but without safeguards against fear.

Multiple Channels, One Direction

The victim is often guided step by step:

- Which account to use
- What amount to transfer
- When to confirm

Instructions are precise.

There is no room for discussion.

This precision feels authoritative.

In reality, it is control.

The Illusion of Oversight

Victims are often told that:

- Accounts are being monitored
- Transactions are visible in real time
- Officers are supervising the process

This creates the illusion of oversight.

The victim believes the system is watching, verifying, protecting.

But no such system exists.

Only the scammer is watching.

Why Victims Keep Paying

People often ask, "Why didn't they stop after the first transfer?"

Because stopping would mean accepting the truth.

That they were deceived.
That the money is gone.
That fear won.

Continuing feels safer than facing that reality.

Scammers exploit this human tendency mercilessly.

When the Money Runs Out

Eventually, something breaks.

The victim's account empties.
Credit limits are reached.
Family savings are exhausted.

Only then does the scam slow.

The scammer senses diminishing returns.

The tone changes.

Promises become vague.
Delays increase.
Communication thins.

The Disappearance

And then, silence.

The call does not connect.
Messages go unanswered.
The number vanishes.

The victim is left alone with the truth.

The Weight of Realization

The realization arrives slowly.

Not as panic—but as heaviness.

Every message is reread.
Every transfer is replayed.
Every warning sign becomes obvious in hindsight.

Shame settles in.

This shame keeps many victims silent.

It is one of the most powerful tools in the scammer's arsenal.

Money Can Be Recovered. Silence Cannot.

The sooner a victim reports the fraud, the higher the chance—however small—of recovery.

But shame delays action.

Victims fear judgment.
They fear blame.
They fear being told what they already know.

This delay benefits only one party.

The True Cost of the Money Trap

The loss is not just financial.

It is trust.
Confidence.
Peace of mind.

Victims begin doubting themselves. Others. Systems. Even reality.

That damage lasts longer than any transfer.

Breaking the Trap

Understanding this trap changes everything.

Money is never verification.
Urgency is never legitimate.
Secrecy is never protection.

No authority needs your money to prove your innocence.

In the next chapter, we will step back and see how this scam looks beyond borders—how the same script appears in different countries, wearing different uniforms, speaking different languages.

Because once you see the pattern globally, it becomes impossible to unsee it.

Chapter 7

Digital Arrest Scams Around the World

For many victims, one detail feels particularly disturbing after the scam ends.

They realize they were not targeted because of who they were—but because of **where they lived**.

Change the country, and the uniform changes. Change the language, and the script adapts. Change the agency name, and the fear remains the same.

Digital Arrest scams are not local crimes.

They are global performances.

Different Countries, Same Fear

The first mistake people make when trying to understand cyber fraud is assuming it is tied to a specific region or culture.

It is not.

What varies across borders is **the symbol of authority**.
What remains constant is **human psychology**.

In every country, scammers impersonate the institutions people fear the most.

Police.
Tax authorities.
Immigration departments.
Customs officials.
Federal agencies.

The scam does not travel with a fixed identity. It adapts.

India: Authority, Reputation, and Fear of the System

In India, Digital Arrest scams often lean heavily on law enforcement imagery.

Victims are told they are under investigation by police, cybercrime units, or central agencies. The language is formal. The tone is stern. The threat is reputational as much as legal.

Many victims fear public humiliation more than punishment.

The scam exploits this deeply ingrained concern.

People are warned that their name will be circulated, that neighbors or employers will be informed, that their family will be questioned.

Silence is framed as dignity.
Compliance is framed as cooperation.

And fear does the rest.

United States: Taxes, Federal Power, and Legal Consequences

In the United States, the script shifts.

Scammers often impersonate federal agencies, tax authorities, or law enforcement bodies with nationwide jurisdiction.

The fear here is less about social shame and more about **financial and legal ruin**.

Victims are told they owe unpaid taxes, that warrants have been issued, or that federal charges are pending. The language emphasizes legal consequences, frozen accounts, and court proceedings.

The urgency is relentless.

Pay now, or face arrest.

The scam relies on the complexity of the system. Most people do not fully understand federal procedures—and scammers exploit that uncertainty expertly.

United Kingdom: Compliance, Formality, and Trust in Institutions

In the UK, Digital Arrest–style scams often adopt a softer tone.

The language is polite. The threat is implied rather than shouted. Victims are told they are "required to cooperate" or "assist with an ongoing matter."

The authority invoked is often related to taxation, immigration, or compliance failures.

British victims frequently describe feeling trapped not by fear alone, but by a sense of obligation.

They believe they must follow rules—even when those rules feel uncomfortable.

Scammers use that instinct.

Europe: Bureaucracy as a Weapon

Across many European countries, scammers exploit bureaucracy.

They reference forms, case numbers, cross-border investigations, and regulatory frameworks. The scam feels complex and official.

Victims feel unqualified to question it.

The more complicated the explanation, the more believable it becomes.

Confusion becomes compliance.

Asia-Pacific: Immigration, Customs, and Surveillance

In parts of Asia-Pacific, Digital Arrest scams often involve immigration and customs authorities.

Victims are told their travel documents are compromised, their visas are under review, or parcels linked to their identity have been intercepted.

These scams are particularly effective among:

- Migrant workers
- International students
- Frequent travelers

The fear of deportation, detention, or blacklisting overrides rational thought.

Scammers know this.

Middle East: Residency and Legal Status

In regions where residency status is tightly regulated, scammers focus on legal compliance.

Victims are told their permits are under review, that documentation issues have arisen, or that violations have been detected.

The threat is not just arrest—but removal.

For many, this fear is existential.

Scammers do not need to raise their voices.

The risk speaks for itself.

Language Is Local. Manipulation Is Universal.

One of the most chilling aspects of these scams is how well they adapt linguistically.

Scammers switch languages effortlessly. They adjust accents. They mirror cultural norms.

They know when to be aggressive.
They know when to be polite.
They know when silence is more effective than threats.

This is not random.

It is practiced.

Organized Crime Without Borders

Despite the local flavor, these scams are rarely local operations.

They are run by organized groups that operate across borders, jurisdictions, and time zones.

Calls may originate in one country.
Money may move through another.
Victims may live elsewhere entirely.

This fragmentation makes enforcement difficult.

Jurisdiction becomes unclear.
Responsibility becomes diluted.
Recovery becomes rare.

And the scam continues.

Why Global Awareness Is Still Low

Despite the scale of the problem, global awareness remains fragmented.

Each country treats these scams as local crimes. Media coverage focuses on domestic cases. Victims believe their experience is isolated.

Scammers benefit from this fragmentation.

They reuse scripts endlessly—because the audience keeps changing.

The Same Ending Everywhere

No matter the country, the ending is the same.

The call ends.
The authority disappears.
The money is gone.

And the victim is left alone with the realization.

Different accents.
Same silence.

Why This Matters

Understanding the global nature of Digital Arrest scams does something powerful.

It removes personal blame.

This did not happen because you misunderstood your country's system.

It happened because the scam was designed to adapt to it.

Once you see the pattern across borders, the scam loses its mystique.

It is no longer personal.

It is mechanical.

Seeing the Pattern Is Protection

The moment you recognize that:

- Every country has its "authority figure"
- Every scam uses fear + urgency + isolation
- Every victim experiences the same arc

The illusion breaks.

And once broken, it cannot be rebuilt easily.

What Comes Next

So far, we have followed the scam from fear to money—and across borders.

Now we must look behind the curtain.

In the next chapter, we will examine who is really behind these scams—not individuals acting alone, but organized networks designed for scale.

Because understanding the structure of the crime helps explain why it is so hard to stop.

And why awareness remains the most powerful defense we have.

Chapter 8

Organized Crime Behind Scams

By the time most victims begin to understand what happened to them, a disturbing assumption takes hold.

They imagine a single person at the other end of the phone—some clever fraudster working alone, improvising, reacting, getting lucky.

That image is comforting.

Because if the crime was individual, accidental, or opportunistic, it feels containable.

The truth is far more unsettling.

Digital Arrest scams are rarely the work of individuals.
They are the product of **organized systems**—designed, refined, scaled, and optimized like businesses.

This is not chaos.

It is structure.

The Myth of the Lone Scammer

The idea of a lone scammer persists because it fits an old narrative of crime: one criminal, one victim, one event.

Digital Arrest scams do not work that way.

They require:

- Scripts tested on thousands of calls
- Technology infrastructure that runs continuously
- People trained for specific roles
- Financial networks to move and clean money

No single person can manage all of this alone.

What victims experience as a personal attack is actually the final step of a long, invisible process.

A Business Model Built on Fear

At their core, these scam networks operate like illicit enterprises.

They have:

- Recruitment pipelines
- Training systems
- Performance metrics
- Hierarchies of authority

The product is fear.
The conversion is money.
The customer is the victim.

Calls are not random. They are targeted by geography, language, time zone, and vulnerability.

Failure is expected.
Success is measured statistically.

Inside the Scam Operation

Most large-scale Digital Arrest scams follow a familiar internal structure.

At the bottom are callers—often young, interchangeable, and trained to follow scripts precisely. They are not improvisers. They are performers.

Above them are supervisors who monitor calls, guide escalation, and decide when a victim is "ready" to move forward.

Higher still are coordinators who manage technology, documents, and identity impersonation.

At the top are organizers—the ones who never speak to victims, never appear on calls, and never touch the money directly.

They design the system.

And systems are resilient.

Training the Voice of Authority

Callers are trained extensively.

They learn:

- How to sound calm under pressure
- How to use pauses effectively

- How to redirect questions
- How to recognize hesitation

They practice responding to doubt.
They rehearse emotional escalation.
They learn when to reassure and when to intimidate.

This training is not accidental.

It is refined through repetition.

Calls are recorded. Outcomes are analyzed. Scripts are adjusted.

Victims believe the scammer is reacting naturally.

In reality, they are following a playbook.

Scripts That Evolve

Scam scripts are living documents.

When a method stops working, it is replaced. When victims become aware of one tactic, another takes its place.

This is why Digital Arrest scams look different today than they did a year ago—and will look different again in the future.

The core principles remain unchanged:

- Authority
- Fear
- Urgency
- Isolation

Only the details evolve.

The Role of Technology Teams

Behind the scenes, technical teams support the operation.

They manage:

- Caller ID manipulation
- VoIP systems
- Video setups
- Document templates
- Messaging accounts

These tools allow scammers to appear local, official, and credible—anywhere in the world.

When an account is blocked, another appears. When a number fails, it is replaced.

Redundancy is built in.

This is not improvisation.

It is planning.

Money Movement Is Never Accidental

One of the clearest signs of organized crime is how money is handled.

Victims are rarely asked to send money directly to a single account.

Funds are routed through layers:

- Temporary accounts
- Intermediaries
- Digital wallets
- Sometimes cryptocurrencies

Each layer adds distance.

By the time the victim realizes the truth, the money has already moved beyond reach.

This level of coordination does not happen spontaneously.

The Use of Human Intermediaries

Many people involved in these networks never speak to victims.

They may be recruited as:

- Account holders
- Payment processors
- Cash handlers

Some know they are participating in crime. Others believe they are doing legitimate work—or are themselves victims of deception.

This fragmentation protects the organizers.

If one link breaks, the chain continues.

Why These Networks Are Hard to Dismantle

Law enforcement faces immense challenges with these scams.

Jurisdictions overlap.
Evidence crosses borders.
Victims are scattered globally.

A call may originate in one country, be routed through another, involve accounts elsewhere, and target a victim in a fourth.

Responsibility becomes blurred.

Organizers rely on this complexity.

Scale Over Precision

These scams do not aim for perfection.

They aim for volume.

Most calls fail. Many victims hang up. Some recognize the scam early.

That does not matter.

If even a small percentage comply, the operation succeeds.

This statistical mindset is central to organized cybercrime.

The scammer is not focused on *you*.

They are focused on *numbers*.

The Emotional Distance of the Organizers

One of the most troubling aspects of organized cybercrime is emotional distance.

The people designing the scam rarely see the damage directly.

They do not witness:

- Panic
- Shame
- Financial ruin
- Emotional collapse

To them, victims are entries on a spreadsheet.

Amounts transferred.
Calls completed.
Success rates calculated.

Distance allows cruelty to scale.

Why Shutting One Operation Isn't Enough

Occasionally, a scam center is exposed or dismantled.

The news offers brief relief.

But the structure survives.

Scripts are copied.
Personnel move.
Operations restart elsewhere.

These networks are not locations.

They are methods.

And methods travel.

The Victim's Place in the System

Understanding this structure matters for one reason above all others.

It removes self-blame.

You were not outsmarted by one person. You were processed by a system designed to manipulate humans efficiently.

That does not make the loss easier—but it makes it clearer.

Breaking the Chain

Organized crime depends on predictability.

Predictable fear.
Predictable obedience.
Predictable silence.

When people talk, report quickly, and share experiences, patterns emerge.

Patterns are dangerous for organized crime.

They expose structure.

Awareness as Disruption

You do not need to dismantle these networks personally.

You only need to disrupt their most fragile element.

The human response.

Every pause.
Every verification.
Every conversation with a trusted person.

Each one weakens the system.

Looking Ahead

In the next chapter, we will return to the human cost of these crimes—through the stories of victims who lived through them and the aftermath that followed.

Because understanding structure explains how the scam works.

But understanding impact explains **why it matters**.

And without that, awareness remains abstract.

Chapter 9

Stories of Victims

Statistics tell us how often cyber fraud happens.

Stories tell us what it does.

Behind every number is a human life interrupted—sometimes shattered—not by violence, but by fear delivered quietly through a screen.

This chapter is about those lives.

1. The Retired Father Who Wanted Peace

Suresh had planned his retirement carefully.

He had worked for more than thirty-five years, saved diligently, avoided unnecessary risks, and built a modest but secure life for himself and his wife. His days were calm now—morning walks, newspapers, phone calls with his children who lived in another city.

When the call came, it felt like a mistake.

The voice was respectful. Formal. It addressed him as "Sir."

He was told that a bank account linked to his identity had been used for illegal transactions. The words frightened him—not because he understood them, but because he did not.

Suresh had spent his life obeying rules. The idea that his name could be associated with crime felt unbearable.

When the caller warned him not to inform his family "until verification was complete," Suresh agreed immediately. He did not want to worry them. He believed silence was responsible.

Hours later, he had transferred most of his retirement savings.

When the call ended and the silence returned, Suresh sat alone at his dining table, staring at the phone that had betrayed him.

He did not tell his wife that night. Or the next day.

When he finally did, weeks later, he cried—not because the money was gone, but because the sense of safety he had spent a lifetime building had disappeared in a single afternoon.

2. The Young Professional Who Thought She Was Prepared

Ananya worked in technology.

She had attended cybersecurity workshops. She knew about phishing emails and fake links. She prided herself on being cautious.

That is why the call confused her.

It did not sound like a scam. It sounded procedural.

The caller used technical language. He spoke about systems, audits, and verification. He referenced digital trails and compliance requirements.

When she questioned him, he answered calmly. When she hesitated, he reassured her.

Ananya stayed on the call because she believed she was evaluating the situation carefully.

She wasn't.

Fear had already narrowed her focus.

By the time she realized something was wrong, she had emptied her savings account and taken a short-term loan—just as instructed.

Afterward, she replayed the call endlessly, trying to identify the moment she should have stopped.

What haunted her most was not the loss of money, but the loss of confidence.

She no longer trusted her judgment.

3. The Business Owner Who Couldn't Afford to Pause

Ramesh ran a small business.

Every day was about decisions—suppliers, payments, deadlines. There was no room for delay.

When the caller told him his accounts were linked to a financial investigation, Ramesh felt panic rise immediately.

If his accounts were frozen, his business would collapse.

The scammer understood this pressure perfectly.

Every instruction was framed as urgency. Every delay was described as dangerous.

Ramesh followed orders because he believed he was protecting his livelihood.

When the scam ended, he lost not only money, but momentum.

Bills piled up. Trust with partners eroded. Sleep became difficult.

Ramesh described the experience later as "being pushed off balance and never fully recovering."

4. The Mother Who Stayed Silent for Her Children

Meera was a single mother.

Her children were her entire world. Every decision she made revolved around their safety and future.

When the caller claimed her identity was connected to a criminal investigation, her first thought was not herself.

It was her children.

The caller warned her that involving family could complicate matters. Meera believed that silence was protection.

She transferred the money meant for school fees and emergency savings because she thought she was shielding her children from danger.

When the truth emerged, Meera felt a crushing guilt.

Not for losing the money—but for believing she had failed as a parent.

She did not report the crime immediately. Shame held her back.

What finally pushed her forward was realizing that silence might allow the scammer to hurt someone else.

5. The Student Who Felt Too Small to Fight Back

Arjun was studying away from home.

He had never dealt with police or legal systems before. Authority intimidated him.

When the caller accused him of being linked to illegal activity, Arjun froze.

He believed that questioning authority would make things worse.

The scammer spoke quickly, confidently, and dismissively—treating Arjun like someone already guilty.

Arjun complied because he felt powerless.

The money he transferred was borrowed.

The debt remained.

What stayed longer was fear.

For months afterward, Arjun panicked whenever his phone rang.

6. The Professional Who Didn't Report for Months

One of the least visible victims of Digital Arrest scams is the silent one.

The person who does not report immediately. Or ever.

They continue working. Smiling. Living.

But inside, something has fractured.

They avoid conversations about money. They become cautious to the point of anxiety. They distrust institutions they once relied on.

Their loss never appears in statistics.

But it shapes their life.

What These Stories Share

Different ages.
Different professions.
Different circumstances.

But the same emotional arc.

Shock.
Fear.
Compliance.
Silence.
Shame.

None of these victims were reckless.

They were human.

The Cost Beyond Money

Money can sometimes be recovered.

Trust rarely is.

Victims describe:

- Loss of confidence
- Anxiety around technology
- Fear of authority
- Withdrawal from others

The emotional cost lingers long after bank balances stabilize.

Why These Stories Matter

Stories break isolation.

When victims recognize themselves in others, shame loosens its grip.

Understanding that this has happened to many—across ages, professions, and countries—restores perspective.

This was not a personal failure.

It was a systemic crime.

Speaking Is an Act of Resistance

Every story shared weakens the scam.

Every conversation breaks the script.

Silence protects criminals.
Stories protect people.

Looking Forward

The next chapter will explore why so many victims delay reporting—and what happens in those critical hours and days after the scam ends.

Because understanding the aftermath is as important as understanding the crime.

And because recovery—emotional and financial—begins with the truth.

Chapter 10

Why Victims Don't Report Immediately

There is a moment after the scam ends that few people talk about.

The phone is silent.
The messages stop.
The authority disappears.

And the victim is left alone with a truth they are not yet ready to face.

This moment—the space between realization and action—is where most victims remain trapped.

Not because they don't know what to do.

But because they don't know how to begin.

The Shock That Freezes Action

The first emotion is not panic.

It is disbelief.

Victims replay the call repeatedly, searching for an explanation that does not involve fraud. They hope the money will return. They expect another call. They believe there must be a misunderstanding.

Reporting feels premature.

"What if this is still real?"
"What if I make things worse?"

Shock suspends action.

Time passes quietly.

Shame: The Strongest Barrier

Shame arrives next.

It is heavy. Personal. Paralyzing.

Victims ask themselves:
"How could I let this happen?"
"What will people think?"
"Will they blame me?"

For educated professionals, the shame cuts deeper. Intelligence becomes a weapon turned inward. The loss feels not just financial, but moral.

Shame convinces victims that silence is safer than honesty.

It isn't.

Fear of Being Judged

Many victims imagine reporting as a public confession.

They picture raised eyebrows.
Dismissive questions.
Implied blame.

They fear being told what they already know: "You should have been more careful."

This fear is often stronger than fear of the crime itself.

So they delay.

Fear of Authorities—Again

Ironically, the very institutions impersonated in the scam become sources of fear afterward.

Victims worry:
"What if I get into trouble?"
"What if they think I was involved?"

The scam has already conditioned them to fear authority.

That fear does not disappear immediately.

The Myth That Reporting Won't Help

Many victims believe reporting is pointless.

"The money is gone."
"They won't do anything."
"It's too late."

This belief is partly true—and dangerously incomplete.

While recovery is difficult, early reporting increases the chance of intervention, alerts banks, and prevents further harm.

Silence guarantees nothing will happen.

Emotional Exhaustion

By the time the scam ends, victims are drained.

They have spent hours—or days—under intense pressure. Their bodies are exhausted. Their minds are foggy.

Reporting requires energy.

Victims often do not have it immediately.

So they rest.

And rest turns into delay.

The Need to Protect Family

Some victims delay reporting to protect loved ones.

They do not want to cause worry.
They do not want to explain the loss.
They do not want to relive the experience.

Silence feels like kindness.

But it isolates the victim further.

When Delay Becomes Dangerous

Every hour matters after a fraud.

Money moves quickly.
Trails fade.
Accounts close.

Delays reduce recovery chances—but more importantly, they allow scammers to continue operating unchecked.

Silence doesn't just hurt the victim.

It protects the system that caused the harm.

Reframing Reporting

Reporting is not an admission of failure.

It is an act of resistance.

It says:
"This happened—and it should not happen again."

Victims who report help expose patterns, warn others, and weaken the scam network.

Even when money cannot be recovered, truth still has value.

The First Step Is the Hardest

Most victims describe the first conversation as the hardest.

Telling someone—anyone—breaks the isolation.

A family member.
A friend.
A bank officer.

Once the story is spoken aloud, shame begins to loosen its grip.

What Victims Need Most

Victims do not need lectures.

They need:

- To be believed
- To be heard
- To be supported

Understanding—not judgment—is what moves people forward.

Turning Pain Into Protection

Many victims eventually report—not because they expect recovery, but because they don't want anyone else to suffer the same way.

This shift is powerful.

Pain becomes purpose.

Silence becomes warning.

A Quiet Truth

Most victims are not weak.

They are wounded.

And wounds heal best when exposed to air—not hidden in the dark.

What Comes Next

In the next chapter, we will move from hesitation to action—laying out exactly what to do when a Digital Arrest scam occurs, step by step, without panic or shame.

Because knowing how to respond is the bridge between fear and control.

And control is what scammers fear the most.

Chapter 11

How to Spot a Scam

How to Spot a Digital Arrest Scam in 60 Seconds

Fear moves fast.

That is why spotting a Digital Arrest scam must be faster.

Victims often say, *"If only I had one clear moment."*
This chapter is that moment.

Not a checklist to memorize.
Not technical advice.
Just **simple recognition**, designed to work **even when fear is high**.

The First 10 Seconds: Listen to the Opening

A Digital Arrest scam reveals itself almost immediately—if you know where to listen.

The caller:

- Introduces authority quickly
- Uses official-sounding language
- Creates seriousness before clarity

Real authorities **do not start conversations this way**.

They identify themselves clearly.
They explain purpose calmly.
They do not rush.

If the opening feels heavy, urgent, or intimidating, pause.

Fear should never be the first tool.

The Next 20 Seconds: Notice the Pressure

Within moments, scammers introduce pressure.

"This is serious."
"This cannot be delayed."
"You must cooperate immediately."

Urgency is not a legal requirement.

It is a manipulation tactic.

Real investigations unfold slowly. They involve notices, documents, and time.

Pressure exists only to prevent thinking.

The Silence Test: Are You Told to Keep Secrets?

This is one of the clearest signs.

If the caller says:

- "Do not tell anyone"
- "Do not contact family"
- "Do not visit the police"
- "Do not consult a lawyer"

The call is not legitimate.

No real authority isolates you from support.

Isolation is how scams survive.

The Authority Illusion: Watch for Performance

Digital Arrest scams rely on performance.

Uniforms on video.
Official-looking backgrounds.
Formal tone.

Authority is acted, not proven.

Real authority does not need to perform.

If someone is *showing* you power instead of *explaining* process, question it.

The Made-Up Term Check

There is no such thing as:

- Digital arrest
- Online custody
- Remote detention

If a term sounds official but unfamiliar—and you are told not to verify it—that is intentional.

Legitimate processes are easy to verify.

Scams rely on confusion.

The Money Moment: The Scam Always Reveals Itself

No legitimate authority will ever:

- Ask you to transfer money
- Ask for “verification deposits”
- Ask for temporary payments
- Ask for secrecy around money

Not once.
Not ever.

The moment money enters the conversation, clarity returns.

Hang up.

The Technology Trap

Scammers use technology to overwhelm:

- Calls
- Video
- Messages

- Documents
- Banking alerts

This is not efficiency.

It is overload.

Overload prevents thinking.

If too many things are happening at once, slow everything down.

The Emotional Signal You Should Trust

Your body often knows before your mind does.

If you feel:

- Sudden fear
- Tightness
- Confusion
- Pressure to obey

Stop.

Fear is not evidence.

It is a signal.

The 60-Second Rule

Here is the truth most victims learn too late:

A real authority will still exist after you hang up. A scam will not.

Take 60 seconds.

Disconnect.
Call someone you trust.
Search independently.

Scammers fear pauses.

One Sentence That Ends Most Scams

You can say this calmly:

"I will verify this independently and call back."

Then hang up.

Do not wait for permission.

No legitimate process punishes verification.

Remember This Above All

No real authority:

- Arrests over phone or video
- Demands secrecy
- Asks for money
- Rushes compliance

Digital Arrest scams collapse under scrutiny.

Your pause is their failure.

Chapter 12

What To Do If You Get a Call

Fear tells you to act immediately.

This chapter asks you to do the opposite.

To pause.
To breathe.
To remember that **control does not belong to the loudest voice on the line**.

If you receive a call claiming you are under investigation, digital arrest, or legal threat, what you do in the next few minutes matters more than anything else in this book.

Not because the danger is real—but because your response determines whether fear succeeds.

The First Rule: Nothing Is Urgent

This may feel impossible to accept in the moment.

The caller will insist that delay is dangerous. They will warn you of consequences. They will suggest that hesitation itself is suspicious.

This is a lie.

Real legal processes do not collapse because you asked for time.
Real authorities do not punish verification.

If someone demands immediate action, urgency is the threat—not the situation.

Step One: Disconnect the Call

This is the hardest step.

Everything in the scam is designed to keep you connected—emotionally and technically. The longer the call continues, the deeper the manipulation goes.

You do not need permission to disconnect.

You do not need to explain.

You do not need to argue.

Simply hang up.

If the call is legitimate, it will survive disconnection.

If it is a scam, it will not.

Step Two: Break the Isolation Immediately

The moment the call ends, speak to someone.

Anyone you trust:

- A family member
- A friend
- A colleague

Do not wait until you "understand things better."

Understanding improves through conversation.

Isolation is where scams grow strongest. Connection is where they weaken.

Say the words out loud:
"I just received a call claiming I'm under investigation."

Hearing yourself say it changes everything.

Step Three: Do Not Verify Using Provided Information

Scammers often offer "verification" paths:

- Call-back numbers
- Email addresses
- Websites

These lead straight back to them.

Never verify a claim using information given during the call.

Instead:

- Look up official contact details independently
- Use government websites
- Call known helplines

Verification must come from **outside** the scam's environment.

Step Four: Understand What Real Authorities Do

When panic hits, clarity matters.

Real authorities:

- Send written notices
- Allow time to respond
- Encourage legal counsel
- Do not demand secrecy

They do not:

- Arrest over phone or video
- Ask for money
- Monitor you constantly
- Threaten immediate consequences

If the call violates these basics, the conclusion is simple.

Step Five: Never Share Financial or Personal Details

No matter how convincing the explanation sounds, never share:

- Bank details
- OTPs
- Account balances
- Identification documents

No legitimate process begins this way.

Once shared, control is lost.

Step Six: If Money Is Mentioned, End the Call

This rule has no exceptions.

No authority anywhere in the world requires:

- Verification deposits
- Temporary transfers
- Security payments

Money demands are the clearest signal.

Do not negotiate.
Do not explain.
Disconnect.

Step Seven: If You've Already Engaged, Stop Now

Many victims think:
"I've already shared some information. It's too late."

It isn't.

Scams depend on continued cooperation.

Stopping immediately limits damage.

End the call.
Block the number.
Do not respond further.

Partial engagement does not obligate completion.

Step Eight: Document What Happened

Once calm returns, write down:

- Time of call
- What was said

- Numbers used
- Instructions given

This helps in reporting and processing the experience.

It also restores a sense of order.

Step Nine: Inform Your Bank (Even If No Money Was Lost)

If you shared any financial information—or felt close to doing so—inform your bank.

Banks can:

- Monitor unusual activity
- Add alerts
- Freeze suspicious transactions

Early notice matters.

Step Ten: Report the Attempt

Reporting does not mean punishment.

It means prevention.

Cybercrime units rely on reports to identify patterns, track methods, and warn others.

Even if no money was lost, reporting strengthens defenses.

You are not wasting time.

You are contributing to awareness.

Managing the Emotional Aftermath

Even if you did everything right, the call may linger.

You may feel shaken.
Embarrassed.
Angry at yourself.

This is normal.

Fear leaves residue.

Talk about it.
Do not minimize it.
Do not dismiss it.

Your reaction does not define your strength.

Your response does.

Teaching Others Without Spreading Fear

One of the most powerful things you can do after such a call is share calmly.

Not with panic.
Not with alarm.
But with clarity.

Explain what happened.
Explain how you responded.
Explain why pausing mattered.

Awareness spreads best through calm voices.

What If the Call Comes Again?

It might.

Scammers reuse data. They retry numbers. They test reactions.

If it happens again:

- Do not engage
- Do not explain
- Do not argue

Silence and disconnection are enough.

A Simple Mental Script to Remember

If fear scrambles your thoughts, remember this:

"I do not act under pressure.
I verify independently.
I do not stay silent."

These three statements dismantle most scams instantly.

You Do Not Need to Be Brave

You do not need courage to handle these calls.

You need permission to pause.

Fear feeds on speed.
Scams collapse under stillness.

The Deeper Truth

Scammers succeed when people believe authority cannot be questioned.

Real safety comes from knowing it can—and must—be.

Hanging up is not defiance.
Verification is not guilt.
Speaking up is not weakness.

What Comes Next

In the next chapter, we will address the most difficult situation of all—what to do **after money has already been lost**, without shame and without despair.

Because recovery is not just about funds.

It is about dignity.

And dignity can always be restored.

Chapter 13

If You've Already Lost Money

There is a moment when hope quietly collapses.

It happens when the call does not come back. When the number no longer connects. When the bank balance refuses to change.

This is the moment most victims remember most clearly—not because of what happened, but because of how alone they felt when it did.

If you are reading this chapter because you have already lost money, know this first:

You are not late.
You are not foolish.
You are not beyond help.

And you are not alone.

The First Emotion Is Often Shock, Not Panic

Contrary to what people expect, the first response is rarely hysteria.

It is stillness.

Victims describe sitting quietly, staring at their phone, replaying conversations word by word. The mind searches desperately for an explanation that does not involve fraud.

"Maybe this is still part of the process."
"Maybe the money will return."
"Maybe I misunderstood."

This is the mind protecting itself.

Shock slows reality so it arrives in pieces.

When Reality Finally Lands

Reality does not arrive with a scream.

It arrives with weight.

A heaviness in the chest.
A tightness in the stomach.
A sense of time stretching strangely.

Victims often say, “I knew then.”

This realization hurts—not only because of the money, but because of what it represents: trust broken, safety violated, confidence shaken.

This pain is real.

And it deserves to be acknowledged.

Stop the Bleeding First

Before thinking about recovery, stop further loss.

If there is any chance that:

- More calls may come
- More instructions may follow
- More money could be requested

End all contact immediately.

Do not respond.
Do not explain.
Do not negotiate.

Scammers rely on continued communication.

Silence is your first protection.

Contact Your Bank Immediately

This step matters—even if you feel embarrassed.

Banks do not judge.
They respond to patterns.

Call your bank's official helpline—not numbers given during the scam.

Tell them plainly:
"I believe I have been a victim of fraud."

Ask for:

- Transaction review
- Account monitoring
- Temporary freezes if needed

Time matters here.

Even if recovery is unlikely, early action improves the odds.

Report the Fraud—Even If It Feels Hopeless

Many victims hesitate here.

They believe reporting is pointless if money cannot be recovered.

This belief is understandable—but incomplete.

Reporting:

- Creates official records
- Helps identify scam patterns
- Protects future victims
- Sometimes enables partial recovery

More importantly, reporting shifts the experience from personal shame to public truth.

You are not confessing failure.

You are documenting a crime.

The Emotional Weight of Shame

Shame often hurts more than the loss itself.

It whispers:
"You should have known."
"You can't tell anyone."
"They will judge you."

Shame isolates.

Scammers depend on this isolation long after the scam ends.

But shame thrives in silence—and weakens when spoken.

Tell one trusted person.

Just one.

Not to explain everything.
Not to justify yourself.
Just to not be alone.

Why Blame Is the Wrong Question

Victims often ask:
"Why didn't I stop?"
"How could I let this happen?"

These questions feel natural—but they lead nowhere.

Better questions are:
"How was I manipulated?"
"What conditions made this possible?"

Blame freezes healing.

Understanding restores movement.

Grief Is a Normal Response

Losing money through fraud can trigger real grief.

Not just for the money—but for:

- Lost security
- Delayed plans
- Altered futures

Grief does not mean weakness.

It means something mattered.

Allow yourself to grieve—without rushing to "be strong."

Strength comes later.

Rebuilding Practical Stability

Once immediate actions are taken, attention turns to the future.

This can feel overwhelming.

Break it into small steps:

- Review finances calmly
- Adjust short-term plans
- Seek professional advice if needed

Do not rush decisions.

Fear created this situation.

Calm will repair it.

What Not to Do After a Loss

In the aftermath, victims are vulnerable.

Be cautious of:

- “Recovery agents” promising refunds
- Services asking for upfront fees
- People claiming insider access

Fraud often follows fraud.

If someone guarantees recovery, step away.

Real recovery is slow, uncertain, and procedural.

Restoring Trust—Slowly

One of the deepest injuries is loss of trust.

In technology.
In authority.
In oneself.

Trust does not return instantly.

It rebuilds gradually—through verification, conversation, and regained confidence.

Be patient with yourself.

Suspicion born of experience is not paranoia.

It is wisdom forming.

Turning Pain Into Awareness

Many victims find healing in sharing—carefully, on their own terms.

Not as warnings filled with fear.
But as lessons grounded in calm truth.

Your experience has value.

It can protect others.

This does not mean reliving trauma endlessly.

It means choosing meaning over silence.

You Are Still Whole

Fraud takes money.

It does not take intelligence.
It does not take dignity.
It does not take worth.

You are still the same person you were before the call.

Wounded, perhaps.

But not diminished.

A Quiet Truth About Recovery

Recovery is not always financial.

Sometimes it is emotional.
Sometimes relational.
Sometimes simply internal.

Peace returns slowly.

But it does return.

What Comes Next

In the final chapters of this book, we will look ahead—at how cyber fraud is evolving, how technology may change the landscape again, and how ordinary people can stay grounded in an increasingly digital world.

Because awareness is not about living in fear.

It is about living with clarity.

And clarity is the strongest defense we have.

Chapter 14

The Future of Cyber Fraud

Cyber fraud is not standing still.

It is learning.

Every time a scam succeeds, it gathers information. Every time it fails, it adapts. Every warning issued, every news article published, every awareness campaign launched becomes part of the environment criminals study and respond to.

The future of cyber fraud will not be defined by one dramatic invention or a single breakthrough technology.

It will be shaped quietly—by refinement, repetition, and psychological precision.

From Opportunistic Crime to Engineered Deception

In the past, many scams relied on chance.

Mass emails. Random calls. Poorly written messages. Obvious lies.

Those still exist—but they are no longer the core threat.

Modern cyber fraud is engineered.

Scripts are tested.
Language is optimized.
Timing is refined.

What once depended on luck now depends on design.

Digital Arrest scams are a clear example of this evolution—not because they are technologically advanced, but because they are psychologically precise.

The future will follow this path.

Artificial Intelligence: Not the Villain, But the Accelerator

Artificial intelligence will not invent cyber fraud.

But it will accelerate it.

AI can:

- Adapt scripts in real time
- Adjust tone based on emotional response
- Translate language instantly
- Imitate accents and speech patterns

This does not mean scams will become unrecognizable.

It means they will become **smoother**.

Less clumsy.
Less obvious.
Less dependent on human error.

The danger is not that AI will outsmart people.

It is that it will **sound reassuring while doing harm**.

Voice Cloning and Familiarity

One of the most unsettling possibilities is voice cloning.

Hearing a familiar voice triggers immediate trust.
It bypasses skepticism.
It feels personal.

In the future, scammers may imitate:

- Authority figures
- Customer service voices
- Even people known to the victim

This does not require perfection.

It only requires familiarity long enough to create confusion.

The response cannot be panic.

It must be verification.

Deepfakes and Visual Authority

Just as voice can be imitated, so can appearance.

Video deepfakes may make uniforms more convincing. Faces more believable. Expressions more authoritative.

But even here, the risk is often overstated.

Deepfakes do not create trust on their own.

Fear does.

A calm, confident person on a screen—real or fake—only becomes dangerous when urgency and isolation are added.

The technology may evolve.

The manipulation remains the same.

Data as the New Fuel

Future scams will rely less on guessing and more on data.

Data leaks.
Public profiles.
Digital footprints.

The more information available, the easier it becomes to personalize deception.

Victims will feel "chosen," not targeted.

This sense of specificity increases credibility.

The defense is not hiding completely.

It is recognizing that **access does not equal authority**.

Scams Will Blend Into Normal Life

One of the most dangerous trends ahead is normalization.

Fraud will increasingly resemble legitimate processes:

- Familiar platforms
- Polite language
- Official-looking workflows

The difference between real and fake will not be obvious at first glance.

This does not mean everyone is at risk all the time.

It means people must rely less on appearance—and more on principles.

Why Technology Alone Will Not Save Us

Many believe better technology will solve cyber fraud.

Stronger security.
Smarter filters.
More automation.

These tools help—but they do not address the core problem.

Fraud succeeds because it manipulates **people**, not systems.

As long as humans experience fear, authority pressure, and urgency, scams will find ways through.

The solution must be human-centered.

The Shift From Awareness to Preparedness

Awareness campaigns often focus on information.

Preparedness focuses on response.

Knowing about scams is useful. Knowing what to do **when fear hits** is essential.

The future belongs to those who can pause under pressure.

That is a skill.

And like any skill, it can be learned.

Institutions Will Adapt—Slowly

Governments, banks, and platforms will continue improving protections.

But systems move slowly.

Fraud moves fast.

This gap will always exist.

That is why individual judgment remains the final line of defense.

Not perfect judgment.

Calm judgment.

The Role of Community

One of the strongest defenses against future fraud is conversation.

Scams thrive in silence.
They weaken in shared awareness.

Families that talk openly.
Workplaces that discuss incidents.
Communities that remove shame.

These environments reduce vulnerability.

The future of safety is not isolation.

It is connection.

Redefining Digital Literacy

Digital literacy is no longer just about using technology.

It is about understanding **how technology can be used against us emotionally**.

This includes:

- Recognizing pressure tactics
- Understanding authority performance
- Accepting that hesitation is healthy

The most digitally literate person in the future will not be the fastest.

They will be the calmest.

Fear Will Always Be the Target

No matter how advanced scams become, one truth remains constant:

Fear will always be the entry point.

Fear of punishment.
Fear of loss.
Fear of shame.

Technology may change the delivery.

It will not change the destination.

What the Future Demands of Us

The future of cyber fraud demands less panic and more presence.

Less speed and more pause.

Less blind trust and more quiet verification.

This is not about becoming suspicious of everything.

It is about becoming grounded.

A Realistic Hope

Cyber fraud will not disappear.

But its power can diminish.

Every informed pause weakens it.
Every calm verification disrupts it.
Every story shared reduces its reach.

The future does not belong to scammers.

It belongs to people who refuse to surrender control under pressure.

Preparing for What Comes Next

As you move into a more digital world, remember this:

Technology changes fast.
Human nature changes slowly.

Scams evolve at the intersection of the two.

Understanding that intersection is your protection.

Looking Toward the End

In the final chapter of this book, we will step away from crime and return to life—how to stay safe, grounded, and confident in a digital world without living in fear.

Because safety is not about constant vigilance.

It is about quiet confidence.

And confidence grows from clarity.

Chapter 15

Staying Safe in a Digital World

By the time you reach this page, you have walked through fear.

You have seen how a simple phone call can dismantle certainty, how authority can be imitated, how money can be extracted, and how silence can deepen the wound. You have also seen something else—less obvious, but far more important.

You have seen that none of this happens because people are careless.

It happens because people are human.

Staying safe in a digital world does not require becoming suspicious of everything or fearful of technology. It requires something quieter and stronger.

Awareness.
Presence.
The willingness to pause.

The Digital World Is Not the Enemy

Technology did not create deception.

It only amplified it.

Long before phones and computers, fraud relied on the same tools: trust, urgency, authority, and fear. The digital world has simply made those tools faster and more scalable.

Blaming technology misses the point.

Technology can also protect, connect, and empower. It allows families to stay close, businesses to grow, and knowledge to spread. The goal is not withdrawal.

The goal is balance.

Safety Is Not Constant Vigilance

Many people respond to cyber fraud by becoming hyper-alert.

They stop answering calls.
They distrust every message.
They retreat from digital spaces.

This reaction is understandable—but it is not sustainable.

True safety is not built on fear.

It is built on **calm discernment**.

Knowing when to engage.
Knowing when to pause.
Knowing when to walk away.

The Power of the Pause

If there is one habit that protects more than any other, it is this:

Pause before responding to fear.

Fear wants speed.
Safety lives in stillness.

A pause creates space between stimulus and action. In that space, clarity returns. Perspective widens. Options appear.

No legitimate authority collapses under a pause.

Only scams do.

Verification Is Not Distrust

Many people hesitate to verify because they fear appearing rude, suspicious, or uncooperative.

This is a misunderstanding.

Verification is not defiance.
It is responsibility.

Real institutions expect verification.
Real professionals welcome it.

Only those with something to hide fear independent confirmation.

Staying Connected Is Staying Safe

Isolation is the strongest ally of fraud.

Connection is its greatest enemy.

Talking openly about suspicious calls, near misses, and even losses builds collective awareness. It removes shame. It spreads practical knowledge faster than any warning poster.

Safety grows in shared understanding.

Teaching the Next Generation Calmly

Children and young adults are growing up in a world where digital interaction is normal.

Fear-based warnings will not help them.

What they need are principles:

- Authority can be questioned
- Urgency should be examined
- Money and secrecy never mix
- Pausing is strength

Teaching these calmly prepares them far better than alarm.

Trust Yourself Again

One of the quiet casualties of cyber fraud is self-trust.

Victims often doubt their judgment long after the event.

Rebuilding that trust matters.

Remember this:
You were not wrong to trust.
You were misled under pressure.

Trust, paired with awareness, becomes wisdom.

Accepting Uncertainty Without Panic

No system is perfect.

There will always be risks.
There will always be attempts.

Absolute safety is an illusion.

But preparedness is real.

Preparedness means knowing how you respond—not controlling everything around you.

A New Definition of Digital Literacy

Digital literacy is no longer just about tools.

It is about understanding:

- How fear affects decisions
- How authority can be imitated
- How silence amplifies harm

The most digitally literate people are not the fastest.

They are the calmest.

Choosing Dignity Over Fear

Fraud tries to strip dignity.

It does this by creating panic, shame, and silence.

Staying safe means refusing to surrender dignity—even when mistakes happen.

Speaking up.
Asking for help.
Learning without self-blame.

These are acts of strength.

What This Book Hopes to Leave You With

Not anxiety.
Not suspicion.
Not fear.

But clarity.

The knowledge that:

- You are not alone
- You are not powerless
- You do not need to rush

Safety is not something granted by systems.

It is something practiced by people.

A Final Truth to Carry Forward

Scams rely on the belief that authority cannot be questioned and fear must be obeyed.

You now know that neither is true.

Authority can be verified.
Fear can be paused.
Silence can be broken.

And in that knowledge lies protection.

Closing Thought

The digital world will continue to evolve.

So will deception.

But so can awareness.

And awareness—quiet, grounded, shared—is stronger than any script.

Stay curious.
Stay connected.
Stay calm.

That is how you stay safe in a digital world.

Chapter 16

Digital Arrest Safety Checklist

Read This Before You React

If You Receive a Call Claiming You Are Under Investigation

Pause. Breathe. Nothing is urgent.

Immediate Red Flags (Even One Is Enough)

If the caller:

- Says you are under digital arrest

- Claims arrest or investigation over phone / video call
- Tells you not to inform anyone
- Creates urgency or fear
- Uses legal terms but avoids clear documentation
- Asks you to stay continuously on the call
- Mentions money, verification deposits, or transfers

It is a scam.

What to Do Immediately

- Hang up the call
- Do not argue or explain
- Do not follow instructions
- Do not share any details
- Block the number

A real authority will still exist after you disconnect. A scam will not.

What Real Authorities NEVER Do

Real police, courts, or government agencies:

- Do NOT arrest people over phone or video
- Do NOT ask for money to prove innocence
- Do NOT demand secrecy
- Do NOT threaten immediate arrest
- Do NOT keep you under constant monitoring

How to Verify Safely

- Speak to a family member or friend immediately
- Look up official contact numbers yourself
- Visit or call a known police station or official website
- Never use contact details provided by the caller

Verification is not guilt. Verification is protection.

If Money Is Mentioned

- End the call immediately
- No authority anywhere in the world asks for:
    - Verification deposits
    - Temporary transfers
    - Security payments

Money = scam. Always.

If You Have Already Shared Information

- Stop all communication
- Inform your bank immediately
- Change passwords and PINs
- Monitor accounts closely
- Report the incident to cybercrime authorities

Stopping early limits damage.

Remember This Under Pressure

- Fear is a tool, not proof
- Urgency is manipulation

- Silence protects scammers
- A pause protects you

You are allowed to pause.

One Sentence That Ends Most Scams

"I will verify this independently and call back."

Then disconnect.

Share This Checklist

- With family members
- With parents and elders
- With colleagues and friends

Awareness spreads fastest through calm conversations.

Final Reminder

There is no such thing as a digital arrest. There is only fear delivered through technology.

Stay calm. Stay connected. Stay safe.

Conclusion

When Fear Loses Its Power

Every Digital Arrest scam begins the same way—with fear introduced suddenly and authority performed convincingly. But every story in this book ends the same way as well: with understanding slowly replacing panic, and clarity returning where confusion once lived.

That is not an accident.

Fear is powerful, but it is not permanent.

What gives cyber fraud its strength is not technology, intelligence, or complexity. It is speed. Urgency. Silence. The moment a person is rushed into believing they must act alone and immediately, fear takes control. But the moment that rush is interrupted—even briefly—the spell weakens.

This book was written to create that interruption.

What Digital Arrest Really Reveals

Digital Arrest scams are not just crimes against money. They are crimes against **trust**.

Trust in authority.
Trust in systems.
Trust in oneself.

That is why their impact lingers long after bank balances stabilize. Victims do not just ask, *"How did I lose money?"* They ask, *"How did I lose control?"*

The answer, as this book has shown, is not stupidity or carelessness. It is **human psychology under pressure**. Anyone placed in the same conditions—fear, authority, urgency, isolation—can respond in the same way. That truth is uncomfortable, but it is also liberating. Because what is human can be understood, and what is understood can be protected.

From Fear to Awareness

Awareness does not mean memorizing every scam or anticipating every threat. That is impossible. Cyber fraud will continue to evolve. Scripts will change. Voices will improve. Technology will advance.

But the *patterns* will remain the same.

Fear will still be used.
Authority will still be imitated.
Urgency will still be weaponized.
Silence will still be demanded.

Recognizing these patterns matters far more than recognizing specific scams. Once you know what pressure feels like, you are harder to rush. Once you know what false authority sounds like, you are harder to intimidate. Once you know that secrecy is a red flag, isolation loses its grip.

Awareness does not eliminate risk—but it transforms outcomes.

The Quiet Strength of the Pause

Perhaps the most important idea in this book is also the simplest:

You are allowed to pause.

No genuine authority punishes verification. No legitimate process collapses under scrutiny. No real investigation requires secrecy from loved ones.

Scammers depend on speed. They cannot survive patience.

The pause—hanging up, calling someone else, taking a breath—is not weakness. It is power reclaimed.

For Those Who Were Harmed

If you were personally affected by a Digital Arrest scam, this conclusion is not meant to tell you to "move on" or "be strong." What happened mattered. The loss mattered. The fear mattered.

But what happened does not define your intelligence, your worth, or your future.

You were targeted because you are human—not because you failed.

Recovery is not just financial. It is emotional. It is the slow rebuilding of confidence, trust, and calm.

And that recovery begins the moment shame loosens its hold and understanding takes its place.

Speaking up, reporting, and sharing experiences are not admissions of weakness. They are acts of resistance.

For Those Who Were Reading to Protect Others

If you read this book to protect your family, parents, colleagues, or friends, remember this: fear spreads fastest through silence, but safety spreads fastest through calm conversation.

You do not need to frighten people to protect them. You do not need to overwhelm them with information.

Sometimes all it takes is one sentence shared at the right moment:

"No real authority will ever arrest you over a phone call."

That sentence has stopped more scams than any technology ever will.

The Future Is Not Hopeless

Cyber fraud will not disappear. But neither will awareness.

Every conversation weakens the script.
Every pause disrupts the process.
Every shared story reduces shame.

Scams thrive in isolation. They shrink in the presence of clarity.

The future does not belong to criminals who rely on fear. It belongs to people who refuse to surrender judgment under pressure.

A Final Reminder to Carry Forward

Before you close this book, remember these truths:

- Fear is not evidence
- Urgency is not legality
- Silence is not cooperation
- Verification is not guilt

And most importantly:

There is no such thing as a digital arrest.

There is only a story told quickly, hoping you will not pause long enough to question it.

Now you know better.

Closing Thought

Staying safe in a digital world does not require suspicion of everything or withdrawal from technology. It requires something far quieter and far stronger:

The ability to stay grounded when fear demands speed.

If this book has given you that—if it has helped you slow down even once—it has done its job.

Stay calm.
Stay connected.
Stay aware.

That is how fear loses its power.

About the Author

Manoj Kumar Nair is a seasoned Information Technology professional with over twenty-five years of experience driving technology transformation across manufacturing and R&D focused organizations. Today, he heads Information Technology for a multinational organization.

Manoj's career spans successes and setbacks, major technology shifts and industry disruptions. From long nights during go-lives, audits, and cyber incidents to leading digital transformations, he has lived the full evolution from "doing IT" to "leading IT."

His writing focuses on simplifying complex technology concepts and presenting them in a way that everyday readers can understand and apply in real life. Manoj's work includes the popular books like ChatGPT & Generative AI, AI Explained Simply, and AI Skills.

www.nairmanoj.com